THE GODPARENT BOOK

THE GODPARENT BOOK

Elaine Ramshaw

LITURGY
TRAINING
PUBLICATIONS

Acknowledgments

Copyright © 1993, Archdiocese of Chicago: Liturgy Training Publications, 1800 North Hermitage Avenue, Chicago IL 60622-1101; 1-800-933-1800, fax 1-800-933-7094; e-mail orders@ltp.org. All rights reserved.

This book was edited by Victoria M. Tufano with assistance from Sarah Huck. It was designed by Jill Smith, typeset by Jim Mellody-Pizzato in Gill Sans and Goudy, and printed in the United States of America.

The illustrations are the work of Anna Horvath.

Library of Congress Cataloging-in-Publications Data
Ramshaw, Elaine, 1956 –
    The godparent book/Elaine Ramshaw.
      p. cm.
    ISBN 1-56854-015-9
    1. Sponsors — United States. 2. Children — United States — Religious life.
    I. Title.
  BV1478.R36 1993   93-29858
  248.8'45 — dc20   CIP

GPBOOK

To my godchildren,
Miriam Adelaide Elsa Schmidt
and
David Evan Williams

Contents

As a godparent, you are called to make room in your life and in your heart for your godchild, and to find ways to help her or him grow up in relation to God. If that sounds too heavy or uncomfortably pious for you, read on!

The basic tasks of the godparent are to remind the child that he or she is baptized and to learn with the child what that means in daily life. This doesn't mean that you're always talking about baptism. When you make God's love real to a child by your own deep appreciation of and delight in and patience with the child, you are communicating to him or her what it means to be God's beloved. In fact, like any spiritual relationship, godparenting is nothing if it's not a genuine human relationship of appreciation and care. If your face lights up whenever you see your godchild, if you take seriously the child's thoughts and feelings, then you may receive the great gift of the child's trust and friendship in return. Then the two of you will be able to witness to the reality of baptism in each other's lives.

If you live far away from your godchild and don't see her or him often, don't assume you can't make a relationship. Even a two-year-old can remember someone she sees only a few times a year, and she can think about that person without any prompting from an adult.

Many of the suggestions in this book are things you can do from a distance or on occasional visits. The very fact that you are an adult who takes a special interest in the child will make you significant to him or her.

All children need adults, in addition to their parents, who take an active interest in their lives and growth in faith. Because the child's parent or parents have invited you to take on this role, they are probably eager that you do so, but be sure that the parents know what you are doing. As you keep open the lines of communication with your godchild, do the same with the parents.

One more thing you might wish to discuss with the parents is the common misunderstanding that being a godparent means that you would be the child's guardian if her or his parents died. This is not true. If the parents want to name you as the legal guardian in the event of their death, they should discuss this with you, and they must make that decision explicit in their wills. If no legal guardian is named, one of the parents' closest relatives usually is granted guardianship. Godparenthood has no legal relationship to guardianship.

Godparenthood is a unique, privileged relationship between two Christians. There are as many ways of being a good godparent as there are people willing to give it a try, and there are sure to be some "godparenty" things that will flow naturally out of who you are and what your godchild is like. This book is not meant to direct that you will do all or most of the things described, but to offer some suggestions for activities that may help you develop your own style of godparenting.

This book was written for use by people in all the churches that have godparents. That means that sometimes it will say "parish" when you would say "congregation," or "the liturgy" when you would say "Mass." Feel free to translate when necessary!

■ Around the Time of Baptism

■

The parents of your soon-to-be godchild probably will meet with their pastor or another minister one or more times before the baptism. These meetings will include a discussion of the liturgy and of the meaning of baptism. Ask if you can participate in these meetings.

■

During the celebration, a baptismal candle will be lit from the large paschal (Easter) candle. Ask if you can supply your godchild's baptismal candle. Ready-made ones can be bought from church-supply stores, but consider making a candle (find a candlemaker or a craft book to tell you how) or decorating a plain candle with colored-wax designs (see page 61 for ideas).

■

In some churches, the child is clothed in a white baptismal garment during the liturgy. If the parents don't have a family baptismal gown, perhaps you could make or help make this garment.

■

Shortly after the baptism, draw one or more pictures of the baptismal event. You may think you that can't draw at all, but try to overcome that resistance. Your purpose is not to produce great art, but to preserve your memories for your godchild. You can use these pictures later in her life to talk to her about her baptism day. The very fact that adults don't usually draw will make this special.

■

Make a little book about the baptism, using pictures you draw, photos taken on the baptism day, the church bulletin and other mementos. Write about your feelings on that day, what you remember and what you understand baptism to mean. This scrapbook can be used to talk with your godchild later about his baptism, and eventually can be given to him.

■

Start a "Growing Up Baptized" book that you will work on together with your godchild. Get a large, blank book (8.5 x 11-inch size is easier to draw in than the 5 x 7-inch size) or a sturdy notebook (art supply stores are a good source for these). Begin the book with your pictures and memories of the baptism day, and add to it every year on the baptismal anniversary or at another yearly event when you will be together. For the first couple of years you'll have to make the entries yourself, saying something about what you want the child's baptism to mean to her this year. By preschool age, your godchild can begin adding a picture every year and including her thoughts (at first dictated, later written herself) about her baptism.

■

Ask the parents of your godchild how they chose the child's name. Find out what other names were considered, what name was planned if the child had been the other sex, and why this particular name was chosen. Is the child named after someone? What is the story behind that? Take note of all this for future conversation with your godchild —kids are usually very interested in the story of their own naming. You can write about this in the memory book you've started.

■ Building a Relationship

■

Think back to your own childhood and adolescence and make a list of the adults whom you trusted and liked to be with, those who made you feel special and appreciated. One way to do this is to draw a timeline of your early life and, next to each year of your life, write in the names of adults who were important to you when you were that age. Then try to identify what those adults did that was helpful to you. Did they do something to make you feel loved or to give you hope or self-respect or a new way of seeing things? Did they help you through a crisis or help you deal with problems or fears? Can you imagine doing the same sort of thing for your godchild? If you feel that you needed certain kinds of help and support that you didn't get, imagine what an adult could have done that would have helped. Could you imagine doing that for your godchild?

■

Set aside some time to do whatever the child wants to do. This may mean joining a preschooler in an imaginative game and following his directions, or taking an older child to a movie or museum of his choice. This kind of time spent with the child tells him that you care about his wishes and feelings as much as your own.

■

Listen to your godchild and take what she says as seriously as you would if she were a grown-up friend. Look at her when she talks, let her finish her sentences, make comments that repeat part of what she said so she knows you're really listening.

■

Look for things to appreciate in your godchild, and tell him what you see. Praise him when he's helpful, kind, brave, creative. If everybody complains about some quality of his, try to find a way to recast it in a more positive light. Never compare him to his brothers or sisters.

■

Tell stories about your own childhood, not "when I was your age" stories that are really disguised lectures, but stories about experiences that might connect to things the child is going through. What scared you, excited you, disappointed you, angered you or interested you when you were your godchild's age? Do the two of you have experiences in common — music lessons, sports, studies, great or horrible teachers, loyal or treacherous friends — that you can compare feelings about?

■

One of the best ways to maintain a relationship with a child of any age is through the mail. Children love getting mail addressed to them, and there are all sorts of inexpensive things you can send through the mail: stickers, bookmarks, comic strips or puzzles cut from the newspaper, riddles and jokes from a children's joke book, funny poems (ask a children's librarian), a homemade puzzle made from a cut-up postcard, or the children's bulletin, if your church has one. You can buy a big paperback book of puzzles, mazes, hidden pictures or whatever your godchild enjoys, and send one page to her every week.

■

When your godchild is old enough to read, you can write letters regularly. One godmother writes her godchild a letter at the beginning of every season of the church year (Advent, Lent, Easter and so on), talking about God, about ways to pray and about issues that are important in the child's life at that moment (this information comes mostly from the mother). For instance, if the child has a friend she keeps getting in fights with, the godmother may write about dealing with conflict in friendships, and about using prayer to collect herself and think about what to do when she's angry. The girl keeps all these letters in a folder and goes back and rereads them often, on her own or with her mother.

■

Instead of just asking your godchild what his favorite sport, subject at school, book or whatever is, try asking "best and worst" questions. What's the best thing and the worst thing about the class you're in this year? What's the best thing and the worst thing about this summer for you? If the child feels like he shouldn't say anything is "worst," ask what his "least favorite" thing is. Asking these double-sided questions is a simple way to let the child know that you're interested in all his feelings, not just the pleasant ones that make adults feel good.

■ Remembering Baptism Together

■ If you can be with your godchild on his baptismal anniversary, you and the family can mark the day with a simple ritual. Light his baptismal candle, say a prayer thanking God for the child and for his baptism, share memories of his baptism using photos or pictures you drew. You might all draw a picture about his baptism. If you are making a "Growing Up Baptized" book with him (page 7), this would be a good occasion for you both to write and draw in the book about what his baptism means to both of you this year.

■ Use images and stories to convey to your godchild what baptism means. Adults often try to explain what a sacrament means by using abstract concepts such as original sin, forgiveness or salvation, but children (and most adults) understand images better. Some of these images may be found in the prayer that your church uses to bless water during the baptismal liturgy. For example, baptism is like a flood washing away all the badness, but not destroying us because God carries us safely in the ark. Baptism is like crossing through the Red Sea from slavery to freedom, with the forces that would enslave us swallowed up in the waters. Baptism is like crossing the Jordan River, being led home out of wilderness wandering into the Promised Land. Telling these biblical stories is one of the best ways to explain what baptism means. It doesn't matter that your godchild won't be able to articulate how sin is like slavery, or how salvation is like homecoming; the stories will give baptism layers of meaning for him if you associate these stories with baptism in the telling.

■

Find images and stories for talking about baptism in children's literature and movies. Dorothy destroys the Wicked Witch of the West by melting her; couldn't this be an image of the power of baptism over witches and monsters? A legend from southern France says that St. Martha tamed the dreaded sea monster, the Tarasque, by sprinkling it with holy water. Martin Luther fended off the devil by proclaiming "I am baptized!" In C. S. Lewis's *Voyage of the Dawntreader*, the scene where Eustace is turned from a dragon back into a boy is clearly an image of baptism. The scene near the end of Mary O'Hara's My

Friend Flicka (also in the movie, available on video) in which Ken holds Flicka all night long in the stream, is a wonderful image of baptism as healing and sacrificial love. Joan Aiken's short story "A Long Day without Water" (in *Haunting Tales*, edited by Barbara Ireson [Dutton, 1974]) is a terrific read-aloud story of communal sin and reconciliation and renewal by flood waters. A story needn't involve water to serve as an image of baptism; for instance, Dr. Seuss's *Horton Hatches the Egg* (Random House, 1940, 1968) tells how the egg was transformed into Horton's child because Horton so faithfully kept his promise to care for it, just as we become God's children by virtue of God's promise-keeping.

■

Whenever you talk about baptism with your godchild, do something to make the discussion more concrete and enjoyable. You can look at the symbols and mementos from the child's baptism day — the candle, baptismal garments, photos, pictures you drew and memories you wrote down (page 6). And the two of you can draw about her baptism together. Such drawings can be literal, depicting what actually took place, or more symbolic. In her book, *Celebrating the Church Year with Young Children* (Novalis/The Liturgical Press, 1988), Joan Halmo suggests that children might draw themselves filled with the light of Christ.

■

Mark the baptismal anniversary by doing something watery together. Go swimming, walk by the ocean, play with boats in the bathtub, run through the lawn sprinkler, visit an aquarium.

■

If you can't be with your godchild on her baptismal anniversary, send her a card to mark the occasion. You may be able to buy a baptismal anniversary card at a church-supply store, or through a catalog such as that of Conception Abbey Press. You can also use a blank card with a picture of a watery scene, such as a photo of a waterfall. Even better, make a card, gluing on glitter or drawing scenes of water or light or cutting pictures out of magazines and pasting them on the card. Don't just sign the card; write a note saying something you remember about her baptism. Or tell her something about what baptism means to you and how much you care about her and how much God loves her.

■

The meaning of baptism is Easter — each baptized person is brought through the cross into resurrection life. So Easter is one of the most important times to talk to your godchild about baptism. If you can't be with her, send her an Easter card and write in it that you always think about her and her baptism especially at Easter, because her baptism means that Jesus' rising from the dead gives her new life, too.

■

Go to the Easter Vigil with your godchild. The Easter Vigil used to be the Mass at which all baptisms took place (many churches still baptize then), and it is the best time to remember our baptism as our own entry into the mystery of the death and resurrection of Jesus. It's also a powerful liturgy for children, because of the darkness and light, fire and water, silence and music. If your godchild's church doesn't have an Easter Vigil, ask his parents if you can take him to one at another church. Or you might want to take him (alone or with his family) to an Easter Vigil at a church other than his own parish simply because the liturgy will be celebrated in a way that will be more memorable and impressive to the child — and to the adults.

■

Take your godchild to an Eastern Orthodox Easter Eve liturgy. Three years out of four, this will take place on a different weekend than Easter in the Western churches. Again, there will be a visual feast of processions and icons and candle-lighting. Both the strangeness of the language and customs and the familiarity of the common symbols will be interesting to many children. These services are late and long, so this will probably be better to do with older children or teens. At the end of the service you are likely to receive an egg dyed red. This will give you the chance to tell the legend of Mary Magdalene explaining the resurrection to Caesar, using an egg as a visual aid to describe Jesus bursting out of the tomb: Caesar said it was as likely that someone would rise from the dead as that the egg in her hand would turn red, which it promptly did!

■

If you and your godchild attend a liturgy at which a baptism takes place, tell him stories about his own baptism. At the baptism of your godchild's younger sister or brother, your task may be to pay special attention to your godchild while everyone else is focusing on the newcomer. Talk to your godchild about how you kept thinking of his baptism, or draw with him about both baptisms.

■

When your godchild receives communion for the first time or is confirmed, see if there are special ways for you to be involved in the event. Some parish programs do involve godparents in some way at these times, by asking the children to communicate with them or by involving them directly in the ritual itself. You might offer to cohost the family's party, if there is one. In any case, you can talk with your godchild about the relationship between communion or confirmation and baptism, and the two of you can draw pictures together about the big event. If you can't be present, try to phone or write, making the connection between this milestone and baptism.

■ Giving Presents

You can be a great godparent without ever giving your godchild a single present if you give him or her your time and attention and affection. But if you want to give presents and would like them to be somehow related to your role as a godparent, here are some ideas.

■

Give watery presents — bath toys, beach or pool toys, squirt toys (animal-shaped squirt toys might be more appropriate than squirt guns), water-sports equipment (from swimming goggles to water skis), bubble bath or fancy soaps. These need not be expensive gifts; plastic kitchen utensils (funnel, turkey baster) can make great bath toys. If you can sew, try making puppets out of washcloths. Tell your godchild that having fun with water is a way of remembering our baptism.

■

Give candles. You can buy candles made in many shapes and colors, or you can make them yourself, or decorate plain, ready-made candles (page 61). The candles you give your godchild need not all be religious designs or shapes; the simple fact that they are candles will be enough for you to make the association to the candle the child received at baptism.

■

Give presents that feature the child's name. Baptism isn't a naming ceremony, but it is usually the time when the child is first called by name in the church. Part of the power of the sacraments is that they take the gospel, which is proclaimed to all the people as a group, and bring it home to each one of us individually. So baptism is, in a sense, about naming; it is the good news that the Shepherd calls each one of us by name. Name presents, whether a simple bookmark you decorate yourself, a bicycle license plate, a carved wall or door decoration, or a piece of jewelry, can be appropriate reminders of baptism.

■

Make a lullaby tape. The most effective lulling is to have the same soothing song sung over and over and over again. You can create this effect on a tape in two ways: You can tape yourself singing the song over and over again, or you can tape yourself singing it once and then, using a dual-tape deck, copy the song several times until one side of a tape is filled. It would be especially appropriate for a godparent to choose a religious lullaby. "All through the night," a favorite lullaby (the first line is "Sleep, my child, and peace attend thee"), is found in many lullaby collections. "Day is done," found in *Worship* (#677), a Catholic hymnal (Chicago: GIA, 1985; third edition) uses the same melody. Other good choices include "Jesus, tender Shepherd," found in *The Hymnal 1940* (#241) from the Episcopal church; "Lord Jesus, since you love me," the second stanza of hymn #282 in the *Lutheran Book of Worship*; and "Thy holy wings, O Savior," #502 in *The United Methodist Hymnal* and #792 in *Hymnal Supplement 1991* (GIA).

■

Make a story tape on which you tell a story yourself or read it from a book. These could be Bible stories, saint stories or readings from books such as those suggested on pages 27 – 28 and in the "Book Suggestions" section.

■

Give a Bible. If your godchild's parents are biblically minded, or if their congregation provides Bibles to children and their families, this may not be necessary. But if no one else provides your godchild with a Bible appropriate for use with and by children, it would be a good thing for you to do. The family should have a Bible that works well for reading aloud by parents or older children; one good choice for this purpose is *A Child's Bible* (Paulist Press). The child herself should have her own copy of the Bible used in the liturgy at her church (the New Revised Standard Version, the New American Bible, or whatever translation is used), and a Bible that is more inviting and understandable to someone of her age. For a fourth grader this might be Sandol Stoddard's *Doubleday Illustrated Children's Bible*, while for an eighth grader the *Good News Bible* (Today's English Version) might be appropriate. *The Living Bible*, which is a paraphrase that is slanted toward conservative Protestant—and anti-Jewish—interpretations, is not recommended.

■
Give younger children picture books based on Bible stories. The very best of these tend to be published by secular presses, which have the resources to pay the best writers and illustrators and to produce beautiful books. Some authors and illustrators to look for are Miriam Chaikin, Tomie de Paola, Marilyn Hirsh, Warwick Hutton, Jane Ray and Peter Spier. You might want to make or buy an accompanying toy to give along with the storybook: a plush lamb with a version of

the parable of the lost sheep, for instance, or a baby doll in a basket with Hutton's *Moses in the Bulrushes* (Atheneum, 1986).

■

Give books that tell the stories of great Christians. There are some picture books of saints' biographies and legends: Tomie de Paola's *Francis: The Poor Man of Assisi* (Holiday, 1990), *Patrick: Patron Saint of Ireland* (Holiday, 1992), *The Clown of God* (Harcourt Brace Jovanovich, 1978) and *The Lady of Guadalupe* (Holiday, 1980), and Margaret Hodges and Trina Schart Hyman's Caldecott Award-winning *St. George and the Dragon* (Little, Brown & Co., 1984). For older children, look in the biographies section of a children's bookstore for age-appropriate biographies of great Christians such as Sojourner Truth. A child will develop his own tastes by the time he is eight or nine, and may like "true stories" or prefer fantasies or mysteries. Find out what your godchild likes to read!

■

Give books that, while not based on the Bible or on the lives of saints, have religious and moral depth. C. S. Lewis's seven *Chronicles of Narnia* have been important in forming the religious imagination of countless children. They are fantasies that include a Christ-figure and a Christian worldview, but they are not at all preachy. (Wonderworks video versions are available through public-radio catalogues.) The books of such authors as Paula Fox, Madaleine L'Engle, Jean Little, Doris Orgel, Katherine Paterson and Mildred Taylor consistently have a spiritual and moral depth to them. Elizabeth George Speare's *The Bronze Bow* (Houghton Mifflin, 1961), which won the Newbery Award, is still the only well-written children's book in which Jesus appears as a character. Robert Cormier's *Bells for Us to Ring* (Dell, 1990) tells of an 11-year-old's questions about religious differences, miracles and the power of God. One good place to look for children's books with a social conscience is the list of books that have won the Coretta Scott King Award (a children's librarian will be able to get it for you).

■

Give recordings of good religious music. Good Christmas recordings are easy to find, but apart from Christmas finding good religious music can be hard. African American spirituals are often attractive to small children, and there are many great recordings of these. Young children may be open to all sorts of genres — folk and gospel and classical and rock and country. Many people assume that small children only like "kiddie" music with simple, repetitive tunes, because such music is the easiest for little ones to learn to make themselves. The truth is that even very small children may appreciate complex or difficult music. One three-year-old girl, who knew plenty of children's songs and lullabies, used to say at bedtime, "Sing 'Alleluia!'," by which she meant the sixteenth-century hymn "Christ is arisen." Older children will develop their own tastes in music, and their tastes should be considered when choosing presents.

■ Praying for Your Godchild

It's important that you pray for your godchild, but there isn't any one right way to pray. You may already pray daily for people you care about; in that case, all you have to do is include your godchild in your regular prayers. But many good Christians haven't found a way to pray that works for them. What follows are suggestions for different approaches to praying for your godchild; maybe one of them will feel right to you.

■

If you'd like to have a special prayer to say for your godchild, you might be able to write one with her help. Ask her, "How do you think we might talk to God about each other? What would you like to say to God about me? What would you like me to say to God about you?" From this discussion, write a simple prayer that includes the things you both want to say. Ask her if the prayer says the important things. Write it out twice and give one copy to your godchild. Tell her that's the prayer you'll pray for her.

■

Many people find it easier to pray when they use an image rather than words alone. Try to come up with some image or picture for what you want God to do for your godchild, for what you hope for her. This image may come from the Bible, the liturgy, hymns, legends or your own imagination. You may picture her held in Jesus' arms, for example, or snuggled under Mary's cloak, or nestled under God's wings, or dancing on the safe side of the sea with Miriam, or standing unscathed in the fiery furnace, or being found by the Good Shepherd, or defeating a monster as St. George or St. Martha did in legend, or simply being surrounded and filled with light. Just picturing her in this way, made safe and strong by the power of God, is a form of praying. The image you use is likely to change over time as your godchild grows older and more active and faces more of the challenges and dangers of the grown-up world. What image seems right this year?

■

If you use an image to pray for your godchild, you may want to try drawing the image, which can be another way of praying it. You may become aware of something in the drawing that you didn't know you were concerned about: The act of drawing can bring to the surface things we push to the background of our minds. If you draw a picture of your prayer image, you might want to show it to your godchild, explaining, "This is what I think of when I pray for you." Doing this could help make your praying a more concrete reality for the child as well.

■

Your godchild's drawings can also serve as a focus for your prayer. Drawings that express his own strong feelings or wishes may give you an image to use in your prayers for him. I once was in an emergency room with a young girl, about seven years old, who was keeping vigil with her family while her grandparent was being treated after a car accident. While she was waiting, she drew a huge, gray castle with a strong iron grate over the entrance, and wrote on the back "For My Family." When I prayed for her later, I asked God to be a mighty fortress for her. If your godchild draws pictures of God, of Bible stories or of other religious images, try meditating with those drawings (or photocopies of them) in front of you. This is one way for your godchild to contribute to your spiritual life; children's drawings often give us new insights into familiar images and stories.

■

If you don't regularly pray outside of church, you may need to find
something that will remind you to pray for your godchild daily or
weekly. Pick something that reminds you of him in a positive way:
the school or firehouse or tennis court you pass on the way to work,
the toy section in the supermarket, or a gift he gave you, for example.
Decide that whenever you see that particular thing you'll pray for
him. Or pick some ritual moment in the Sunday liturgy when you will
pray for him: during the intercessory or congregational prayers, or
right after you receive communion, or when you walk past the font.

■

Another way to pray for your godchild is to make something for her,
and to think about her needs and gifts while you make it, thanking
God for her and telling God what you hope for her. It doesn't matter
what it is you're making; the task simply provides the opportunity to
focus your thoughts on the person you're doing it for. Making a gift
for someone is an act of love and therefore a form of prayer.

■

When some major life event or crisis occurs in your godchild's life,
ask that a prayer for him be included in the prayers at the Sunday
liturgy (For Lisa's godchild Michael, whose family is moving this

week . . .). Some parishes have books for members' prayer intentions. These books are kept in a place where anyone can write their own intentions and read and pray for the intentions of others. These prayers may be included in a general prayer in the liturgy.

■

Ask that your congregation regularly (at least yearly) include prayers for all the members' godchildren, perhaps on the feast of the Baptism of the Lord.

■ Sharing Thoughts and Values

■

Drawing pictures together is a good way to communicate with pre-school or grade-school children. A child often may be able to say what's important to her in a drawing even when it's something she wouldn't be able to put into words. If you draw along with her, the two of you are meeting on the same level. Draw an important event that just happened or will soon happen; or your favorite and least favorite thing about a holiday (Christmas, Easter, your birthday), about church, about what you do all day (school, work); or the members of your family as animals; or your worst and best dreams; or the three wishes you would make if you found a genie; or yourself in the future. With older children, design stained-glass windows with symbols of things that are important to you, or design coats-of-arms for your-selves. For other ideas, check out the series of *Anti-Coloring Books* by Susan Striker and Edward Kimmel (H. Holt and Co.,); you can order these through any full-service bookstore (look in the "Authors" volumes of *Books in Print* under Susan Striker).

■

Try communicating with your godchild through puppets. Children are often inhibited in talking directly to adults, especially adults they don't know well, but they frequently will speak freely to a puppet. Younger children will speak directly to your puppet; older children will be able to create a puppet character to speak for them (a way of making it safe to say things adults might disapprove of). You can make puppets out of paper bags or socks, or borrow some puppets from someone who has them. If you and your godchild really come to enjoy using puppets, you can make an inexpensive puppet theater by putting a suspension rod in a doorway and draping material over it to hang to the floor.

■

Reading a story aloud creates a splendid opportunity for talking about all sorts of subjects that come up. Stories about friendship and betrayal, prejudice and peacemaking, birth and death exist even in picture-book form for small children. When you talk with your godchild about these things, don't ask abstract questions about a concept like "prejudice." Instead, ask concrete questions in terms of the story.

What do you think about what X did to Y? What would you have done? How do you think Y felt about it? Be careful not to sound like you're quizzing, or looking for the one right answer; show real interest and respect for the child's view of things.

■

Television shows, movies and videos also can be used in the service of communication. Pick worthwhile ones, and then watch and discuss them together. Watching a video together can be a particularly good conversation starter with a teenager. In addition to discussing the characters and events in the movie, teenagers will be able to look more critically at how the movie portrayed adults, teens and children; what it says about women's and men's roles; what position it takes with regard to the choices made by the characters.

■

The Ungame is designed to help people share their feelings, memories and wishes in a nonthreatening and enjoyable way. The game provides an opportunity for people to respond, if they wish, to such questions as "If you could be invisible, where would you go?" and questions about what angers them or how they would want to be remembered. Other players cannot talk while a person is talking, or even comment right after; this makes people listen to each other instead of countering or correcting. Players can comment on or ask about each other's responses only if they land on a space that allows them to do so. There are many sets of question cards for the Ungame, each geared at a different age group or at intergenerational groups, and including one set with religious questions. Most children enter into this game easily and enjoy playing it. The question cards can be used independently of the board game, and work well as a travel game on car trips, in hotel rooms and on lines in airports.

■

There are a number of other board games that are designed as formats for sharing thoughts and feelings. LifeStories, like the Ungame, involves question cards that elicit stories, with an accent on memories and family stories. Not So Scary Things, for ages four to eight, lets children act out everyday fears and confidence-building solutions, with a strong element of humor. My Homes and Places, for ages four to fourteen, has question cards for each of the places pictured on the game board: homes, courthouse, school, church, clubhouse, fantasy castle and haunted house. For example, at the haunted house the questions are about scary things, at the church they focus on God and religious differences. These last two games are available from the Animal Town catalogue (PO Box 485, Healdsburg CA 95448-0485; 800-445-8642).

■

Some board games serve as a way to focus on values and moral deci-
sion-making. Scruples poses moral dilemmas, and the players guess
how each other would respond. Two noncompetitive, values-oriented
games are available from Family Pastimes, a company that makes
some of the best cooperative board games (RR4, Perth, Ontario,
Canada K7H 3C6): Together, in which players work together to solve
world and human problems presented in a simplified way, and
Choices, a moral dilemma game of discussion and evaluation.

■

Talk to your godchild about God. This could be especially important
for godfathers, because men are less likely than women to talk about
religion outside church. According to one study of young people
who are involved in the church, most said their fathers rarely or
never discussed religion with them. To start a conversation, you might
focus on the metaphors we use for God. How is God like the sun?
How is God not like the sun? How is God like a father, a mother or a
friend? How is God not like a father, mother or friend? How is God
like a shepherd or a king? How is God not like a shepherd or a king?
Asking both sides of the question helps a child see that all our names
for God are only partially true at best, and helps open the field for
the imagination. Two picture books that raise the issue of how God is

more and other than what we typically imagine are Robert Munsch's *Giant* (or *Waiting for the Thursday Boat*) (Firefly Books, 1989), a humorous tale in which both the giant and St. Patrick find out that God is not quite what they expected God to be; and Douglas Wood's *Old Turtle* (Pfcifer-Hamilton, 1992), a book for older children that describes how all the animals imagined God in some sense in their own image, and how they were all both right and wrong.

You might also ask your godchild what she thinks God has to do with friendships, food, illness, wars. Tell her what you think, but do not correct her opinion. Feel free to tell her there are things you're not sure about, things you don't understand. Two books that can help you see how children think about God and how you might approach the subject with them are John Hull's *God-Talk with Young Children* (Trinity Press International, 1991) and David Heller's *Talking to Your Child about God* (Bantam, 1988).

■

Take your godchild to religious services at other churches, synagogues or other places of worship. Call first to find out whether visitors are welcome and what outsiders can and cannot participate in. Would there be anyone who could answer a young visitor's questions? Talk with your godchild afterward about the service. What seems to be important to these people? How is their worship like ours and different from ours? At some churches, he will be surprised most by the similarities to his own church. One Catholic undergraduate who attended a Lutheran worship service as part of a religion course reported that it was just like a Catholic Mass only they sang all the verses of everything! This can be a good activity to do with teenagers who are interested in comparing belief systems and have enough historical understanding to think about the origins of different religious groups.

■

One way to share values is to talk about whom you want to give money to. You might want to set aside a certain percentage of the money you will give to charitable causes every year, and let your godchild decide where that money will go. For a younger child, you could provide three options of causes she could understand; an older child or teenager could be allowed to choose any nonprofit organization. This gives the child a chance to tell you which causes concern her most, and it also gives her the experience of making yearly decisions about giving money away.

■ Making Sunday Special

■

If you live close enough to your godchild to have regular Sunday visits, do something with her that she particularly likes to do and keep it as a special treat for Sundays.

■

Noah's ark sets used to be called "Sabbath toys" because on Sundays children were allowed to play only with toys that had a biblical theme. Provide a Sabbath toy for your godchild — a Noah's ark set; a set of handpuppets with a shepherd, sheep and wolf; or another toy with a biblical theme. Suggest to the parents that this toy be stored during the week and taken out only on Sundays. The point is not to deprive the child during the week, just as we don't deprive ourselves by not having the Christmas tree up all year. The point is to make Sunday special.

■

Make or buy some small, quiet toys to be used as "church toys," which the preschool child can hold and play with during the liturgy. These will work best if they are put aside to be used only for church; they may also then give him a positive association with going to church. When my nieces were little they loved their doll-muffs (where the muff forms the doll's skirt), which were worn only to go to church.

■

Make a cloth activity book for the preschool child to play with in church. Use buttons, snaps, pockets and other hands-on items to make activity pages involving Christian symbols (Noah's ark, baby Moses in a basket, shepherd and sheep, five loaves and two fish, chalice and loaf of bread, for example).

■

Give your godchild a copy of Gail Ramshaw's *Sunday Morning* (Liturgy Training Publications, 1993), a children's liturgy book that describes simply what is happening in the various parts of the eucharistic liturgy and links each part with an image from a Bible story.

■ Keeping the Church Year

One good place to start looking for ideas about keeping the church year with your godchild is Joan Halmo's book, *Celebrating the Church Year with Young Children* (Novalis/The Liturgical Press, 1988). She explains the meaning of the different seasons of the church year and suggests many activities appropriate for small children, from simple crafts to seasonal music to spontaneous dance-processions through the house. Some of the suggestions in this section are inspired by Halmo.

Advent

■

Make an Advent wreath together. If your godchild's family doesn't have one, she could use this one at home; otherwise, you could use it yourself, or the two of you could give it to someone who doesn't have one (perhaps an elderly, homebound person). An Advent wreath can be made simply with four candle holders, fresh evergreens and a circular form (a sponge form from a florist works best; a bent coat hanger also will work). Traditionally, three of the candles for an Advent wreath are purple, and the fourth candle, lit for the first time on the Third Sunday of Advent, is rose. Because many congregations use blue for vesture and decoration during Advent in addition to or instead of purple, you may prefer to use blue candles. White candles also are fine.

■

Make a new, paper Advent calendar every year and give or send it to your godchild. One advantage to this is that, instead of just counting from December 1, you can make the calendar for exactly the dates Advent covers in the year you make it (from the first Sunday of Advent, which may be in November, to Christmas Eve). Use two large pieces of paper of the same size. Cut the right number of doors in one of them for the days in Advent, and label them with the appropriate dates. Glue it to the other sheet of paper. Open the doors to draw or write something inside each one. Messages can be personalized; you might want to find out dates of importance to the child during Advent (e.g., the day school lets out), so you can refer to those in your messages.

■

Make a permanent Advent calendar. I made one for my godchild that told biblical history leading up to Christ's birth. The hanging is made out of felt, with a felt Christmas tree at the top and 24 pockets at the bottom. The tree has 24 hooks sewn on (Velcro would work, too), and in each pocket is a symbol of a person or event from the Old Testament. These are arranged chronologically, and one is hung on the felt tree each day. I also included in each pocket a small piece of paper that explains the symbol and tells a little of the related scripture story. Using this calendar year after year helps a child learn the outline of biblical history. The events and people I included are listed here with the symbol I used for each.

1. Creation/sun ■ 2. Fall/apple ■ 3. Flood/rainbow ■ 4. Abraham/star ■ 5. Hagar/well ■ 6. Isaac/ram ■ 7. Jacob/ladder ■ 8. Judah/lion ■ 9. Joseph/rainbow coat ■ 10. Moses/basket ■ 11. Miriam/tambourine ■ 12. Sinai/tablets of the law ■ 13. Joshua/trumpet ■ 14. Deborah/palm tree ■ 15. Ruth/wheat ■ 16. David/lyre ■ 17. Solomon and the Temple/incense ■ 18. Elijah/pitcher ■ 19. Hosea/wedding rings ■ 20. Isaiah and the Exile/branch ■ 21. Ezra and the Return/scroll ■ 22. John the Baptist/scallop shell ■ 23. Mary/bee ■ 24. Jesus/baby

■

If you decide to buy an Advent calendar, consider the wonderful

Advent-through-Baptism of the Lord calendar, "Fling Wide the Doors," produced by Liturgy Training Publications. It has special doors for Sundays as well as doors for every date; sometimes you get to open more than one door in a day. It comes with a booklet of prayers for the opening of each door. Of the Advent calendars available in most card shops, choose one that is scriptural (and avoid the ones called "Countdown to Christmas"!).

■

Help your godchild make her Christmas presents (write stories or poems, draw pictures, sew or do crafts you both enjoy). Or take her shopping to buy her presents for others; decisions about what to buy and how much to spend can be occasions to discuss values and perhaps to raise questions about consumerist hype. What are presents really for?

Christmas

■

Give your godchild a nativity set of his own, one that's designed to be played with: a sturdy wooden set, a soft-sculpture set or a set of hand- or finger-puppets. Most traditional nativity sets have no women other than Mary; if your godchild is a girl, look for a set with a shepherd-girl or some other figure she can identify with. You may be able to add this to the set yourself.

■

It is a Spanish tradition to include all sorts of creatures in the manger scenes to show that Jesus came to bring salvation to all the world. You could add a new animal to your godchild's (or her family's) nativity set each year. You might even take requests — "What animal would you like to have come to the manger this year?" One boy had dinosaurs visiting the baby Jesus. He didn't think dinosaurs actually coexisted with Jesus; he knew very well they lived long before humans. This practice helps keep the manger scene from being thought of as merely a historical recreation of something that happened long ago, and turns it into a symbol of everything we care about being blessed by this birth.

■

Commission your godchild to draw designs for your Christmas cards. Take some of the money you would otherwise spend on cards and pay him to draw you a Christmas picture. Have him use a dark marking pen or crayon, or something else that will photocopy well. Photocopy the drawing onto colored paper and fold it to use as a card. Or you can print your Christmas letter under the design.

■

In some places, it is customary to bless the home on Epiphany in memory of the visit of the Wise Men to the Christ child. This can be done by singing an appropriate song, reading the gospel story of the visit of the Wise Men (Matthew 2), and marking the lintel of the door (with chalk) with the year and the initials of the traditional names of the Wise Men — Caspar, Melchior and Balthasar (19+C+M+B+95). Say a prayer for protection, for hospitality and for peace, then go from room to room sprinkling water. Perhaps the Wise Men from the family's manger can join in the procession.

Between the End of the Christmas Season and Ash Wednesday

■

Go outside on a clear night and look at the stars together. Stars are an important symbol in this time after Epiphany, not just because of the star the Wise Men followed, but also because they stand for the light of Christ shining in the world's darkness, enabling us to find our way as we follow him. When you look at stars together, ask a young child what she thinks is out there and share with her what you think. Show a school-age child how to use the Big Dipper to find the North

Star; tell her about how people have used that star to find their way at night for centuries, because it doesn't move like the others. (Can you explain why? She'll ask.) Tell her about sailors using the North Star to steer their ships, and about slaves using it to escape to the North. Talk about how that's like the light of Christ, who can always be counted on to help us find our way.

■

If you can't go outside at night to view the stars, you might be able to go to a planetarium, and have some of the same discussion about Jesus as the star who lights our night and helps us find our way.

■

Give or read to your godchild books that tell the story of slaves finding their way north to freedom by using the North Star. Two good picture books that tell this story are Jeanette Winter's *Follow the Drinking Gourd* (Knopf, 1992) and F. N. Monjo's *The Drinking Gourd* (HarperCollins, 1970). (Monjo's book is for beginning readers and gives more historical context than Winter's.) Talk about how Jesus is like a North Star for us, showing us the way to freedom; you can connect this to the pillar of fire that led the Hebrew slaves at night as they were escaping from slavery in Egypt.

■

With an older child or teenager, look at the book *Powers of Ten* by Eames, Charles and Ray (Scientific American Press, 1982). This is a wonderful book about the sizes of things in the universe. It starts with people on the beach of Lake Michigan, and pulls back from them to show the city, the region, the globe, the solar system, the galaxy; then it goes inside a person's hand to show blood vessels, DNA molecules and so on, down to subatomic particles. It also comes on video and can be ordered through a bookstore, or you might be able to find it through a library or a friendly science teacher. The video is especially good at evoking awe at the size of creation. Either viewing the video or reading the book can be used as an occasion to talk about humanity's place in creation, about how God cares for us in particular, so small among all those stars. The mystery of the incarnation, God's coming in person to enlighten all humankind, is at the center of this time of year.

Lent

■

Around Ash Wednesday, make ashes in a fireplace or a barbecue, and play with the ashes together (wear old clothes!), making crosses or other signs on each other. Include other members of the child's family in this, if they're game. Ask your godchild what ashes make her think of, and talk with her about why we use them in church on Ash Wednesday. Read or tell the creation story from Genesis 2 and 3, where God makes the human being out of the dust of the earth.

■

Go for a lenten walk or hike together (Lent is a time for journeying). If you live in a place where the land seems dead and barren in March, look together for places where new life is hidden. Can you find buds on the branches? Where might animals be hibernating?

■

Plant seeds or bulbs together. Jesus said that a seed must fall to the ground and die to bear fruit (John 12:24). You can explain that though the seed doesn't really die, it's a picture that helps us understand the connection between giving your life and finding it. Tulips and daffodils and lilies have served as Easter symbols in part because they grow year after year from bulbs that look lifeless. If this is not a good time to plant bulbs in the ground in your part of the country, find a book that tells you how to "force" bulbs to bloom inside at Easter.

■

Make pretzels together, or make them yourself and send them to your godchild, or go out to buy fresh, hot ones. Pretzels were first made in the fifth century as a lenten bread (made with no dairy products, as was the rule in Lent), and the traditional pretzel shape was meant to suggest prayer, because in those days people crossed their arms over their chests when they prayed.

■

Talk with your godchild about ways to save the planet. Many older children and teens know a great deal about ecology and are very concerned about what we're doing to the environment. Your godchild will probably be able to suggest ways that you can change your patterns to be less wasteful or polluting. Ask her advice, and tell her you'll try it out this Lent. Reducing our consumption for the sake of the planet is a sort of lenten discipline that will make sense to a teenager.

■

Make palm crosses on Palm Sunday. If you can be with your godchild on that day, show him how to make them (if you don't know how, find someone to teach you). If you're not together, make one and send it to him in the mail.

■

On or around Holy Saturday, read your godchild (tape it if you can't be with her) the slave narrative "Carrying the Running-Aways," found in Virginia Hamilton's *The People Could Fly* (Alfred A. Knopf, 1985; you'll find it in a children's library). The narrator describes rowing across the Ohio River to freedom, guided by a beacon set up by a Quaker on the Ohio side. The scene is like the Easter Vigil: the dark night, the tall light shining by the water in the font. The story of escape from slavery is like the main resurrection image used at the Vigil, the story of the Israelites crossing the Red Sea. Talk about how this is what baptism means: that we go through the water to freedom and life. Talk about the light of Christ, the paschal candle, being the beacon that leads the way, as the pillar of fire led the Israelites.

■

Watch a sunrise together. If it's going to be cold, bring plenty of blankets and hot drinks.

■

Dye eggs together any time during the Easter season. Use some technique of egg decorating other than the one your godchild uses at home. Perhaps you could even learn a new technique each year. Some are simple enough to use with very small children. Joan Halmo (see page 48) suggests three simple methods: (1) Make designs on the egg with crayons or pieces of masking tape before dyeing. (2) After dyeing, make designs with liquid glue and, after letting the glue dry slightly, lay on yarn. (3) Add one tablespoon of vegetable oil to each cup of dye, and dip the egg in one color after another.

Older children can make onion-skin eggs (my favorite): Wrap a raw egg in the skins of yellow onions, then wrap a scrap of white or colorfast material around the egg to keep the skins next to the egg, and then tie the whole package up with string. After you hardboil the wrapped eggs and let them cool off, cut away the string and cloth; you'll find golden-brown eggs with individual patterns from the onion skins. Give the eggs to someone who will appreciate them (perhaps an elderly neighbor, or someone who lives alone and who doesn't dye eggs).

■

Make a special Easter bread with or for your godchild. Children especially like the braided Easter breads with the colored eggs set into them. Recipes for such breads can be found in many bread cookbooks; they're not much harder to make than any other yeast bread.

■

Decorate candles with or for your godchild. Get thin sheets of colored wax, cut them into whatever shape you want and press them onto the candle. You can also decorate a candle with thin pieces of brightly colored paper cut into shapes. These can be affixed to the candle in two ways: by using a hot-wax gun, or by pressing the edge of the paper with a hot knife (the adult does this for a young child). If you don't see your godchild at Easter, you might want to make and send her a new candle with Easter and baptismal symbols every year at that time.

■

Eat a meal together by candlelight.

■

Go for an Emmaus walk. This is an Easter Sunday or Monday tradition in much of Europe; you can do it any time during the Easter Season. A walk in the country or in a park and ending with a picnic is a way to remember how two people met Jesus as they walked and how they recognized him at their meal.

■

Use the symbol of the butterfly as a way to express the resurrection life of Easter. This is an especially good symbol for small children.

Make origami butterflies or fly a butterfly kite. Help the child act out the transformation from caterpillar to butterfly: He can curl up inside a sleeping bag for a chrysalis or cocoon, then dress in a butterfly costume of paper or cloth wings you've painted or colored together. Give butterfly toys, suncatchers, jewelry, stickers or books (Eric Carle's *The Very Hungry Caterpillar* for a toddler; nature books for older children) as Easter gifts. If you and your godchild both like butterflies, you can do a different butterfly activity every Easter.

■

Take a young child to visit a petting zoo.

■

One Sunday of the Easter Season is Good Shepherd Sunday, when the gospel lesson tells how Christ is like a shepherd. You might do things related to the symbol of the shepherd at this time, to help make that image come alive for your godchild, who probably doesn't see shepherds in her daily life. If you live anywhere near sheep farms or ranches, you might be able to meet a real shepherd so your godchild can ask how they take care of their sheep. Otherwise, you can share children's books about modern shepherds, such as the lovely picture book *The Shepherd Boy* by Kim Lewis (Four Winds Press, 1990), or, for older children, Ester Wier's *The Loner* (Scholastic, 1963,

1991), in which a migrant orphan boy is taken in by a woman shepherd on a ranch. Both books give a detailed, realistic picture of a shepherd's work and care for the sheep.

Many young children enjoy acting out the parable of the lost sheep with paper, wooden or modeling-clay figures of the shepherd and sheep (which you can make with or for them). You might give your godchild a plush lamb and tell her that she is "Jesus' little lamb," but also that she is a good shepherd, like Jesus, when she takes good care of people or animals.

■

See the "Remembering Baptism Together" section for more activities appropriate for this season.

Between Pentecost Sunday and the Beginning of Advent

■

Summer and fall are good times for all sorts of outdoor activities: walks, picnics, hikes and camping. The appreciation of growing things can be related to our own growth and to the theme of many of the scripture readings during this time: the growth of the reign of God. What things grow gradually and predictably? What things grow in spurts? What things grow by transforming from one thing to another? What things grow exponentially? Which ways are we growing? In what ways does the reign of God grow? These questions can come up while taking a walk in the country, gardening outside or indoors, or performing science experiments. If you can shop at a farmers' market together, see if one of the farmers will answer your godchild's questions about how the different plants grow and what it was like raising these crops this year.

■

When the school year ends and begins, talk or draw with your godchild about beginnings and endings. Recognize the positive and negative sides of both endings and beginnings. Pay special attention to this in the years when he is moving from one school to another (for example, from grade school to middle school or junior high). What will he miss? What does he anticipate with fear? What does he look forward to with excitement? How would he like you to pray for him during the week he starts at his new school? You might want to say to him that baptism keeps us safe through all the endings of our lives.

■

Many of the parables Jesus told are read in church during this time of the year. Find ways to explore parables with your godchild. Read them to her from the Bible, from a children's Bible or from a good picture book version. Tomie de Paola's *The Parables of Jesus* (Holiday, 1987) is a very good collection. The inexpensive Arch Book series includes some parables, notably Janice Kramer's retelling of *The Good Samaritan* (Concordia, 1964). Unfortunately, two other parables she retold for the same series, *The Rich Fool* and *Eight Bags of Gold*, are out of print. Another good picture book based on a parable, also out of print, is Regine Schindler's *The Lost Sheep* (Abingdon, 1981). These books are worth looking for in your public or church library; if they aren't available locally, ask your librarian if they are available through interlibrary loan. Eric Carle's *The Tiny Seed* (Picture Book Studio, 1990) is not meant to be a version of a parable, but it tells a story that is much like the parable of the tiny mustard seed becoming the greatest of bushes (Mark 4:30 – 32).

■

Make up some new parables (this means you have to figure out what sorts of stories parables are). Or identify experiences either you or your godchild has had that were like real-life parables. For example, I once arrived at a theater at the last minute due to a terrible winter storm. When my friend and I looked around for seats, we couldn't find any that were empty except for the front row of the second section — prime seats — which was roped off with a "Reserved" sign.

Without much hope we went to the usher, and she led us right to those seats. She told us that they were reserved for latecomers so that they could be seated without disturbing others in the audience. We not only got great seats, we got them *because we were late!* The reversal that happened here was a lot like what happens in many of Jesus' parables, where the annoying woman gets justice, the straying sheep gets all the shepherd's attention, and the prodigal son gets the big party. Have you ever found yourself in the middle of a parable?

■ Godparenting in Times of Crisis

There are many different sorts of crises that your godchild might be faced with as he or she grows up. This section gives some general advice applying to all sorts of situations, followed by a few explicit suggestions for what to do if your godchild experiences a geographical move, the death of someone close or the divorce of his parents.

■

When your godchild is faced with any crisis, educate yourself about what this might be like for her, what she might be feeling. Ask a teacher who works with children that age, a nurse, a children's therapist, or, if the crisis is a death, a funeral director (many of them are excellent grief counselors). Or contact people in a support group dealing with this sort of crisis situation. For instance, if your godchild's baby brother dies, you might talk to someone from a support group of parents who have had an infant die, and ask them about siblings' grief. Or if your godchild tells the family she is a lesbian and that is very hard for you to come to terms with, you might contact a support group of families and friends of lesbians and gays. Such support groups can usually be found in an urban newspaper's Sunday activities listing. Another way to educate yourself is to find a good book that describes for parents or adult helpers what a particular crisis is like for children. Most librarians would be able to find an appropriate book for you.

■

Provide your godchild with books written for children his age who are coping with the situation he faces. There are books available for children who are adjusting to a new baby, moving, experiencing their parents' divorce, entering into a stepfamily, grieving, coping with their own serious illness or addiction or the illness or addiction of a family member, and so on. You could give such a book to your godchild, or read it to him in person or on a tape.

■

Talk with your godchild about the crisis, at the time and later. Draw with her about it. Ask "best and worst" questions: What times are hardest? What helps the most? Answer her questions honestly, giving her the facts as she can understand them. If she's too young to understand some important element of the situation, promise you'll talk to her about it again when she's older. Then do so.

■

Keep as much continuity as you can in your relationship with your godchild. In a time of crisis, it can be very reassuring to have some aspect of life remain unchanged. This means continuing your patterns of contact with him through a move or divorce (or instituting new ways to do some of the most important things), but it also means little things, like greeting your godchild in the same way as usual on your first visit after his baby sister is born, rather than going first to look at the baby.

When someone close to your godchild dies

■

Learn what you can about how a child this age experiences death. Two helpful books for adults caring for grieving children are Theresa Huntley's *Helping Children Grieve* (Augsburg, 1991), which also discusses the grief of dying children, and Helen Fitzgerald's *The Grieving Child: A Parent's Guide* (Simon & Schuster, 1992). *Helping Children Cope with Death* by Hannelore Wass and Charles Corr (Hemisphere,

1984) has an annotated bibliography of books for adults concerning children's grief.

Children will experience most of the same feelings as grieving adults, but there are three important ways that children's grief differs from that of adults. First, a child experiencing a certain feeling may look quite different from an adult experiencing the same feeling. For example, a depressed child may become hyperactive, or a child overwhelmed by unmanageable feelings of sadness and fear may get very angry, lashing out at those near to her. A child who just heard of a parent's death that morning may play tag in the afternoon; this does not mean that she is carefree or unaffected by the death.

Second, a child's grieving process is complicated by her lack of understanding that death is universal and permanent. How can she come to terms with the "never again" of death if she really can't understand finality at this age? Young children may go on denying the reality of death — or escaping into a fantasy life where the dead person is coming back — far longer than adults can.

Third, children's grief will continue in stages all through their childhood and adolescence, especially when it's a parent who dies. When they come to understand that the loss really is forever, they will grieve anew. When they reach an age at which they need the parent in a new way, they will grieve for that additional loss: the loss of what a father might do and be for a teenaged girl, for instance.

■

Talk or draw with your godchild about his loss. Encourage his questions. Answer them honestly, giving as clear an explanation as possible for the child's level of understanding. Most of the time, what the child imagines will be far worse than the truth. Avoid euphemisms ("we lost Aunt Carol"; "he's gone away"). Don't compare death to sleep; the child may become afraid of going to sleep. Explain what happened to make the person's body stop working.

■

Tell your godchild that it's okay to feel all sorts of feelings. Tell her you have a lot of the same feelings (if you do); let her see you express them. Tell her that other kids who've had a parent, brother or best friend die feel the same things she's feeling. Books may help convince her of this (see page 76), but children's support groups are often the best way for a child to learn this. If the feeling she expresses is inappropriate guilt over the death, let her know that most people have such feelings when someone dies; but make it clear that the death was in fact not at all her fault — a simple, accurate explanation of the cause of death can help alleviate the fear that "I made it happen."

■

Help your godchild participate in the rituals that follow a death. Someone should describe to him, clearly and thoroughly, what will happen during the funeral and burial, what he will see, what people will do, what he can say when people tell him they're sorry. Fitzgerald's *The Grieving Child* has a very good description of how to prepare a child for the rituals (pp. 87–89). You may be able to do this yourself; if not, check to see whether someone else is doing it. Each child should have at least one adult keeping track of him or her during the rituals, an adult who is not overwhelmed with grief and who can pay attention to what the child is feeling and answer the child's questions (But how will he breathe in there?) without breaking down. If you're not overwhelmed by your own grief and you have a close relationship with your godchild, you might be the one who can do this. Someone also should ensure that there is a role for the child in the rituals, if he wishes to have one. He might want to place a drawing or a symbolic gift in the coffin, or write a poem to be read at the wake or funeral. You may be able to help arrange for this to happen.

■

Later in the mourning process there often is a need for some informal rituals for everyone, but especially for children. You might be in a position to suggest or help plan and bring about such rituals. For example, on the first Christmas after the death, the family and friends might gather for a home memorial service. Each person can be asked to bring a symbol of the person who died, and all can show the symbols and share memories. Such a ritual has helped many families both to continue the work of grief and to find a way to celebrate Christmas while acknowledging the painful absence. In some cases, a ritual might be helpful many years after the death: For example, a teenager whose mother died when she was five may now have a need to remember her, to construct a more real picture of her and to mourn the mother she needs as she becomes a woman.

■

Share with your godchild beliefs about resurrection and the life to come. Ask him what he thinks and imagines. But don't bring up God in the explanation of the death if you don't also mention God at other times as the source of life and all we love and value. Don't talk about the death as "the will of God." Rather, emphasize God's presence with us in our suffering and grief, and God's promise of healing and new life in the world to come. Jesus felt as lonely and sad and full of questions (Why have you forsaken me?) as the grieving person does. Easter tells us that even so, Jesus was not finally abandoned, and we won't be, either.

■

Give or read to your godchild books that relate to the kind of loss she has experienced. It's harder to find the right books for a grieving child than for a child who's moving or adjusting to a new brother or sister because the circumstances of death and grief are so varied. A children's librarian or a person who works with grieving children may help you find appropriate books. For a small child whose grandparent has died, a picturebook such as Joan Fassler's *My Grandpa Died Today* (Human Sciences Press, 1971) or Jane Resh Thomas's *Saying Good-bye to Grandma* (Clarion Books, 1988) may be paths into conversation. For an older child or teen whose parent has died, nonfiction books such as Jill Krementz's *How It Feels When a Parent Dies* (Knopf, 1982), a collection of children's and teens' first-person accounts of their parents' deaths, or Eda LeShan's *Learning to Say Goodbye: When a Parent Dies* (Macmillan, 1978) may be helpful and reassuring. Hannelore Wass and Charles Corr's *Helping Children Cope with Death* (Hemisphere, 1984) has an excellent annotated bibliography of books for children.

If your godchild's parents separate or divorce

■

Keep as much continuity as you can in your relationship with your godchild. If you've been involved in holiday rituals with him, try to continue those rituals in the new situation, but talk openly about the fact that the holiday feels very different now. Be constant in the patterns the two of you have developed of talking and doing things together. If the divorce brings a move, the child's relationship with you may be one of few that continue relatively unaffected by the divorce. That could make the patterns of relating the two of you share all the more precious at this time.

■

Don't take sides. Even if the cause of the separation was wholly one-sided (for example, if a now-absent parent was cruel or violent), the child may need to believe that her parent really cares about her. Answer questions honestly, but don't paint a parent as all bad or completely unloving, for example, "I think he loves you, but he doesn't know how to take care of a child."

■

If you are a closer friend or relative of the noncustodial parent, the custodial parent may try to keep you from seeing your godchild. Don't write off your relationship with your godchild. Let some time go by, and then ask the custodial parent what kind of relationship she or he would be comfortable with. If she or he doesn't want you to see the child, ask if you can write to each other. Tell the parent you respect all she or he is doing for the child and that you want to support that, not undermine it. If she or he still says no to any contact, say that you'll abide by that decision and check back in a year.

When your godchild's family moves

■

Help your godchild say goodbye to the old house or apartment with a ritual. If you live close by or can visit, you can help plan and bring it about; if you're far away, you can suggest it to the child himself or to some adult in the family. The family and other invited guests can go through the house room by room, stopping in each room to share stories of what happened there. Special places in a yard (garden, play corner) may be included in the tour. When the tour is complete, people might be asked what they will miss most about the house and what hopes they have for the house's future and for their own future in their next home. A good way to end such a ritual is with a party-style meal; the gratitude, loss and hopes expressed can be summed up in prayer at the meal.

■

Suggest or help organize a house blessing for the new apartment or house. Your denomination may have a printed liturgy for house blessings; the Lutheran and Episcopal books of occasional services both have one, as does *Catholic Household Blessings and Prayers*. These usually involve walking from room to room and pausing in each room to read an appropriate Bible passage and say a short prayer. Children should be given an active role, doing some of the reading or carrying a candle or a bowl of blessed water to sprinkle around.

The Epiphany tradition of marking the doorways with the year and the initials of the Three Kings might be adapted as a home blessing (see page 54). Children often enjoy having permission to write on walls, and you can plan a short inscription that makes sense to you — perhaps just a cross and the date. You might conclude this ritual with a festive meal, perhaps a house eucharist.

■ Godparenting the Grown-up Godchild

The major responsibilities of godparenting are carried out while the godchild is growing up; but the relationship need not end when the godchild turns 18. The nature of the adult-to-adult relationship will, of course, depend on what you have built over the years. Whether you can talk easily about God and faith will depend partly on whether you've done so all along, and partly on what the adult godchild's attitude is toward God, the church and matters religious. If he distances himself from the church, don't push religious language or expectations; try to stay connected personally in a positive way. Your continued caring will be a witness to him of grace even if he shies away from any mention of God.

■

Continue writing letters to your godchild at least once a year. Talk about what baptism means to you as you enter midlife, as you age.

Comment on the good things you see in her especially over the past year — the personal growth, admirable qualities. Many adults can't remember the last time they were praised by an older adult, yet grown-ups also need to be affirmed by the older generation.

■

In letters or in conversation, share some of the struggles and adventures of your adult faith journey. Did your faith play a role in major decisions of your life — deciding whether to change jobs, whether to begin or end a relationship, or whether to have children? Has your faith changed in times of crisis or loss? How have you struggled with moral dilemmas? You might share these experiences when your godson or goddaughter is facing a similar issue.

■

Give gifts that help an adult make his or her own traditions, rituals and prayer life. When he starts his own household, you might give presents for the ritual life of the home. One woman gave her godson a tablecloth and candlesticks for his wedding, with a note about the importance of making meals special. Many of the things this book suggests doing for or giving to a young godchild could also be appropriate when an adult godchild is raising his own children: giving an Advent calendar or wreath, or making a lullaby tape, for example.

There are books to help families build their own rituals; especially good is *Rituals for Our Times* by Evan Imber-Black and Janine Roberts (HarperCollins, 1992).

■

Write to your godchild at times of transition in her life: when she moves, when she changes jobs, when a significant relationship ends, when she graduates or earns some professional certification, when one of her parents dies. Recognize the importance of the ending in any transition, even the happy ones. What does this have to do with baptism? In baptism we die with Christ, so that we might be united with his resurrection life, now and in the world to come. Part of the promise of baptism is a promise that God's love will accompany us through all the transitions of our lives. All our losses, all our endings, all the little deaths of our lives are drawn into the cross, and through the cross into Easter. The Easter promise is not that things will come out all right in this situation, but that God will give us safe passage. In African American churches, sometimes the pastor proclaims "God will make a way," to which the congregation responds, "where there is no way!" In the fiery furnace, in the Red Sea, in the wilderness, even in the tomb, the God of our baptism will join us and give us safe passage.

■ Book Suggestions

Books make wonderful gifts for godparents to give to their godchildren. This list offers some suggestions, but there are many good books that are not on this list. Consult a children's librarian, a teacher or the owner of a good bookstore for other suggestions.

Throughout this book, I have recommended a number of books and games that might be helpful to you as a godparent. At the time this book was written all the books recommended here and in the text were in print, except where otherwise noted, but that situation can change quickly. Any book that is in print can be ordered for you at any bookstore worthy of the name. Give the person the author and title (and the publisher, if you know it). If the book is listed in *Books in Print*, the store can order it for you. Virtually any book in or out of print can be obtained through one library or another. If your local public, school or university library doesn't have a copy of the book you want, the librarian usually can get one for you through interlibrary loan.

Christmas Picture Books

Buckley, Ray. *The Give-Away*. Nashville: Abingdon, 1999.

Humans have lost their way, and the animals try to help them by giving some precious part of themselves; but finally God must give away power and safety to come to humanity as a vulnerable baby. Draws on the Native American practice of the ceremonial give-away as a metaphor for God's self-sharing in Jesus.

dePaola, Tomie. *The Clown of God*. San Diego: Harcourt Brace Jovanovich, 1978.

An old juggler gives his last performance before the statue of the Madonna and Child as his gift to the Christ child.

_____. *The Legend of the Poinsettia*. New York: G. P. Putnam's Sons, 1994.

A Mexican legend of the poinsettia, where a girl who has no gift for the Christmas procession brings weeds, and the leaves turn red. Available in Spanish or English.

Hoffman, Mary. *Three Wise Women*. Illustrated by Lynne Russell. New York: Phyllis Fogelman Books (Penguin Putnam), 1999.

Three women, from Europe, India and Africa, visit the Christ-child after the wise men. They bring bread, a story, and the love of a child.

Langstaff, John. *What a Morning! The Christmas Story in Black Spirituals*. New York: Macmillan Children's Book Group, 1987.

Christmas spirituals printed with their music and with striking illustrations.

Nussbaum, Melissa Musick. *The Winter Saints*. Illustrated by Judy Jarrett. Chicago: Liturgy Training Publications, 1998.

Stories of saints and others follow the season of winter, the days of Advent and the twelve days of Christmas.

Root, Phyllis. *All for the Newborn Baby*. Illustrated by Nicola Bayley. Cambridge, Massachusetts: Candlewick Press, 2000.

A book reminiscent of a medieval illuminated manuscript, with a rhyming lullaby text that draws on many legends of various creatures' gifts to the baby Jesus.

Rosen, Michael. *Elijah's Angel*. Illustrated by Aminah Brenda Lynn Robinson. San Diego: Harcourt Brace Jovanovich, 1992.

Elijah Pierce, the renowned African American woodcarving artist, makes an angel for a Jewish boy, who wonders if it's all right for him to accept a Christmas angel. A story of Jewish/Christian respect and friendship.

Vivas, Julie. *The Nativity*. San Diego: Harcourt Brace Jovanovich, 1988.

It's very hard to illustrate the story of the nativity with surprising freshness, but Vivas succeeds. The pictures are down-to-earth and magical, humorous and reverent.

Wilner, Isabel. *B Is for Bethlehem*. Illustrated by Elisa Kleven. New York: Dutton Children's Books, 1990.

A rhyming alphabet book that tells the Christmas story with joyful, colorful collage illustrations.

Books for Easter

Gibbons, Gail. *Easter*. New York: Holiday House, 1989.

The story and symbols of Easter for young children.

Gragston, Arnold. "Carrying the Running-Aways." In Virginia Hamilton's *The People Could Fly*. New York: Alfred A. Knopf, 1985.

A story that goes with the Easter Vigil: an exodus from slavery across water in darkness, guided by a tall beacon.

Hamilton, Virginia. *Many Thousand Gone: African Americans from Slavery to Freedom*. New York: Alfred A. Knopf, 1993.

True stories of slavery and exodus; good reading for Holy Week.

Houselander, Caryll. *Petook: An Easter Story*. Illustrated by Tomie dePaola. New York: Holiday House, 1988.

A rooster's-eye view of Jesus' life, death and resurrection.

Kimmel, Eric. *The Birds' Gift: A Ukrainian Easter Story*. Illustrated by Katya Krenina. New York: Holiday House, 1999.

A legend of the first Ukrainian Eastesr eggs, the thank-you gift from a flock of golden birds who were saved from freezing one harsh winter by a hospitable town. The town priest welcomes the birds into the church, and preaches about a time to come when all creatures will live in peace.

Nerlove, Miriam. *Easter*. Niles IL: Albert Whitman & Co., 1989.

The best first book on the meaning of Easter for a toddler. The rhyming text follows two children as they celebrate Easter by decorating and hiding eggs and by going to church; the Easter story is told briefly. (The family depicted is African American.)

Nussbaum, Melissa Musick. *Bible Stories for the Forty Days*. Illustrated by Judy Jarrett. Chicago: Liturgy Training Publications, 1997.

A story from the Bible for each day of Lent is wonderfully retold and delightfully illustrated.

Polacco, Patricia. *Chicken Sunday*. New York: Philomel, 1992.

Eula is grandmother to two children and honorary grandmother to their friend. The children make and sell pysanky eggs to buy her a new hat to wear when she sings the solo in church on Easter.

———————. *Rechenka's Eggs*. New York: Philomel, 1988.

A woman rescues a wounded goose. After it breaks the eggs she spent all winter decorating, a small Easter miracle occurs.

Rock, Lois. *Sad News, Glad News*. Illustrated by Louise Rawlings. Colorado Springs, Colorado: Lion Publishing, 1997.

Tells of Jesus' death and resurrection with rhyming text and repeated phrases that engage small children.

Wildsmith, Brian. *The Easter Story*. New York: Alfred A. Knopf, 1993.

The best picture book of the events of Jesus' passion, death and resurrection, with glorious paintings, focusing on the grandeur of the story rather than the pain. Even the scene of the crucifixion is full of angels.

Bible-story Picture Books

Bryan, Ashley. *All Night, All Day: A Child's First Book of African-American Spirituals*. New York: Atheneum (Macmillan Children's Book Group), 1991.

Spirituals with their music, and wonderful illustrations of biblical images; the "welcome table" may be the best picture of heaven in any picture book anywhere.

Chaikin, Miriam. *Esther*. Philadelphia: Jewish Publication Society, 1987.

_____. *Exodus*. New York: Holiday House, 1987.

dePaola, Tomie. *Noah and the Ark*. San Francisco: Harper & Row, 1985.
Includes cut-out finger puppets.

Figley, Marty Rhodes. *The Story of Zacchaeus*. Illustrated by Cat Bowman Smith.
Grand Rapids, Michigan: Eerdmans, 1995.
A faithful and energetic retelling of the story from Luke, a great picture of conversion for children.

Gerstein, Mordicai. *Queen Esther the Morning Star*. New York: Simon &
Schuster, 2000.
The vivid illustrations are full of humor and drama, and help to convey clearly the somewhat complicated plot of the story of Esther. (If you can't get this one, the next best version of Esther is Rita Golden Gelman's *Queen Esther Saves Her People*.)

Hartman, Bob. *The Edge of the River*. Illustrated by Michael McGuire. Wheaton,
Illinois: Victor Books, 1993.
A wonderfully evocative retelling of the story of the baby Moses and Pharaoh's daughter, using concrete detail to draw the reader into the feelings of the sister who was keeping watch over the baby.

Hoffman, Mary. *Parables: Stories Jesus Told*. Illustrated by Jackie Morris. New York:
Phyllis Fogelman Books (Penguin Putnam), 2000.
Retellings by the author of *Amazing Grace* of eight parables, suitable for grade-school children.

Kassirer, Sue. *Joseph and His Coat of Many Colors*. Illustrated by Danuta Jarecka. A Ready-to-Read Book, level 1. New York: Aladdin Paperbacks (Simon & Schuster), 1997.

The story of Joseph for beginning readers, with distinctive (and colorful!) illustrations.

Ladwig, Tim, ill. *Psalm Twenty-Three*. New York: African American Family Press, 1993.

The Shepherd Psalm is illustrated with scenes from the lives of inner-city children, showing the people that guide and care for them in the midst of constant danger.

Orgel, Doris, and Ellen Schecter. *The Flower of Sheba*. Illustrated by Laura Kelly. A Bank Street Ready-to-Read Book, level 2 (Grades 1-3). New York: Bantam, 1994.

For early readers, a retelling of a Jewish legend about how Solomon proved his wisdom to the Queen of Sheba by his willingness to learn from a tiny bee.

Ray, Jane. *Noah's Ark*. New York: Dutton Children's Books, 1990.

Beautifully illustrated, with an ecological emphasis.

Rock, Lois. *Best-Loved Parables: Stories Jesus Told*. Illustrated by Gail Newey. Minneapolis: Augsburg, 1998.

Retellings of seventeen parables which stick closely to the biblical text.

Sanderson, Ruth. *Tapestries: Stories of Women in the Bible*. Boston Little, Brown and Company, 1998.

Stories of thirteen women from the Old Testament and eleven from the New, with pictures resembling tapestries.

Spier, Peter. *The Book of Jonah.* New York: Doubleday, 1985.

   The most interesting and accurate picture-book version of this story.

Wildsmith, Brian. *Exodus.* Grand Rapids, Michigan: Eerdmans, 1998.

   A richly illustrated telling of the story of the Hebrews leaving slavery in Egypt, being cared for in the wilderness, and being given the law.

Arch Books
The Arch Books are paperback versions of Bible stories, published by Concordia Publishing House (St. Louis, Missouri). They range from very good to very bad, so read a book before you buy it. They can be found in many Christian bookstores, and they can be ordered through any full-service bookstore. Of those currently in print, some of the best are:

Hill, Dave. *The Boy Who Gave His Lunch Away.* Illustrated by Betty Wind. 1967.

Kramer, Janice. *The Good Samaritan.* Illustrated by Sally Mathews. 1964.

_____. *The Princess and the Baby.* Illustrated by Sally Mathews. 1969.

Janice Kramer's *The Rich Fool* and *Eight Bags of Gold* (the parable of the talents) unfortunately are out of print, as is another highlight of the series, Mary Warren's *The Great Surprise* (the story of Zacchaeus). You should be able to get these by interlibrary loan.

Picture Books on the Nature of God

Fitch, Florence Mary. *A Book about God*. Illustrated by Henri Sorenson. New York: Lothrop, Lee & Shepard, 1998.

The text, originally published in 1953, was reissued with new illustrations. It uses analogies from nature to suggest what God is like: "The sea that stretches on and on far beyond our sight, /The sea that on the surface moves as it will /But deep down is quiet and still and full of mystery. /God is like the sea."

Sasso, Sandy Eisenberg. *God's Paintbrush*. Woodstock, Vermont: Jewish Lights Publishing, 1992.

Invites children to encounter God through moments in their own lives, and provides adults and children with questions for wondering together about the nature of God. A great conversation starter for people who feel awkward trying to talk with children about God.

_____. *In God's Name*. Woodstock, Vermont: Jewish Lights Publishing, 1994.

Persons all come up with different names for God out of their own experience; finally, looking into God's mirror together, they see God in each other's names for God, too.

Walters, Julie. *God Is Like . . . Three Parables for Children*. Illustrated by Thea Kliros. Colorado Springs, Colorado: WaterBrook Press (Random House), 2000.

Metaphors from nature, explored from a child's point of view, for the three persons of the Trinity: rock for "God our Father," light for Jesus, wind for God's Spirit.

Wood, Douglas. *Old Turtle*. Duluth MN: Pfeifer-Hamilton, 1991.

The different animals all picture God in their own image; Old Turtle shows them how they are all both wrong and right.

Stories for Older Children and Teens Dealing with Religious Questions

Blume, Judy. *Are You There, God? It's Me, Margaret*. New York: Bradbury Press, 1970.

Margaret, with a Jewish father and a Christian mother, has not been brought up in any faith tradition, but she has questions about God.

Howe, James. *A Night without Stars*. New York: Atheneum (Macmillan Children's Book Group), 1983; Avon, 1985.

Twelve-year-old Maria, in the hospital for a heart operation, makes friends with Donald, a boy abused by his mother and disfigured by a fire. Maria struggles with her own faith and wonders where God is in Donald's life.

Langton, Jane. *The Astonishing Stereoscope*. New York: Harper & Row, 1971; Harper Trophy, 1983.

Through time travel, a group of children follow the evolution of religious understanding; one of the scenes they see is the Last Supper.

Lewis, C. S. *The Chronicles of Narnia* (series). New York: Macmillan, 1950–1956.

The Narnia books are imaginative Christian fantasies, full of adventure and humor and vivid characters. Lewis was a theologian, and the books include a Christ figure (Aslan the lion) who dies and rises, a creation story, and a vision

of heaven — but they are not preachy allegories, and they rarely fall into moralism. Lewis wrote the first book for his godchild, Lucy! The seven books in the series are:

The Lion, the Witch and the Wardrobe
Prince Caspian
The Voyage of the Dawn Treader
The Silver Chair
The Horse and His Boy
The Magician's Nephew
The Last Battle

Paterson, Katherine. *Bridge to Terabithia*. New York: HarperCollins Children's Books, 1977.

The death of a boy's best friend raises religious questions for him. This book won the Newbery Medal.

————————. *Jacob Have I Loved*. New York: HarperCollins Children's Books, 1993.

A girl spends her growing-up years in the shadow of her talented and beautiful twin, and she feels even God has forsaken her. Another Newbery Medal winner.

Rylant, Cynthia. *A Fine White Dust*. New York: Bradbury Press (Macmillan Children's Book Group), 1986; Dell, 1987.

Pete's religious search seems to have found a clear answer when the Preacher Man comes to town. Pete's struggle through belief and betrayal to a wiser faith is powerfully portrayed. A Newbery Honor Book.

Speare, Elizabeth George. *The Bronze Bow*. Boston: Houghton Mifflin, 1961.

A boy at the time of Jesus who has reason to hate the Romans must decide between the paths of vengeance and reconciliation. He finds out that love is both harder and more powerful than hatred. A Newbery Medal winner.

Books and Other Materials from Liturgy Training Publications

Erspamer, Steve, illustrator. *An Advent Calendar: Fling Wide the Doors*.

A three-dimensional Advent calendar that covers every day from November 30 until January 6. Comes with a booklet of prayers for each of these days.

Jarrett, Judy, illustrator. *Blessings and Prayers*.

A prayer book for toddlers to primary-grade children, this book contains prayers for morning and night, for meals, for remembering the dead and for praising God.

Jarrett, Judy, illustrator. *40 Days and 40 Nights: A Lenten Ark Moving toward Easter*.

Much like an Advent calendar, the ark has windows for each day of Lent and the Triduum. A booklet with prayers for each day is included.

Ramshaw, Gail. *Sunday Morning*. Illustrated by Judy Jarrett.

The words and phrases used in the Sunday liturgy are linked with Bible stories by playful illustrations and a few brief sentences.

A video made from the book is also available.

■ Remember

My Godchild's Name _____

Date of Birth _____

City _____

Parents' Names _____

Date of Baptism _____

Church _____

City _____

Minister _____